Festival of the Sun

Written by Jong-soon Jo
Illustrated by Sinae Jo
Edited by Joy Cowley

big & SMALL

High up in the Andes Mountains,
Yana lived in a small village close to Cuzco.
Soon, Cuzco was to hold the Festival of the Sun.
The people in the village were curious.
Who would be the king of the festival?
This year, Yana's father
had been nominated for the king.

Cuzco is a city located north-east of the Andes Mountains. It used to be the capital of the Inca Empire.

Pablo shouted to the other children,
"Yana's dad is one of the nominees
for the king of the Festival of the Sun."

"No way!" someone teased.
"He'll never get to be the king."

Yana didn't say a word.
She was offended by the remark
but she kept silent.

When school finished, she ran home.
Mom welcomed her with a huge smile.
"Your dad will be king of the festival!"

"Really?" She jumped up and down.
"Oh! I knew he would be chosen!"

Then her mother said, "I need you
to do a chore for me, Yana.
Take this grilled corn to Usco.
He is shearing the alpacas."

Yana was so excited, she ran.

Alpacas are animals related to camels.
They have soft hair and are raised
by the indigenous people in the Andes
Mountains. Hair from the alpacas
is used to make fabric.

6

Yana's brother Usco
was shearing a young alpaca.

"Usco, I have some corn for you.
Is there anything I can do to help?"

"You can help by staying still,"
said Usco to his sister.

Yana felt grumpy.
She grumbled to herself
and ate some of the corn.

Mom was sitting at her awana.
Next to it were dyed alpaca threads.
Soon the threads would be changed
into cloth for warm clothing.

Yana asked, "Mom, can I help?
I want to learn how to weave."

"You'll learn when you are older,"
said Mom. "Now, go and play."

Yana felt very grumpy.
She stamped out of the house.

An awana is a wooden loom used for making cloth.
Long threads are tied to a wooden frame. This is
the warp. Then threads are woven through them
sideways. This is the weft. The cloth is woven
to the size of the garment needed.

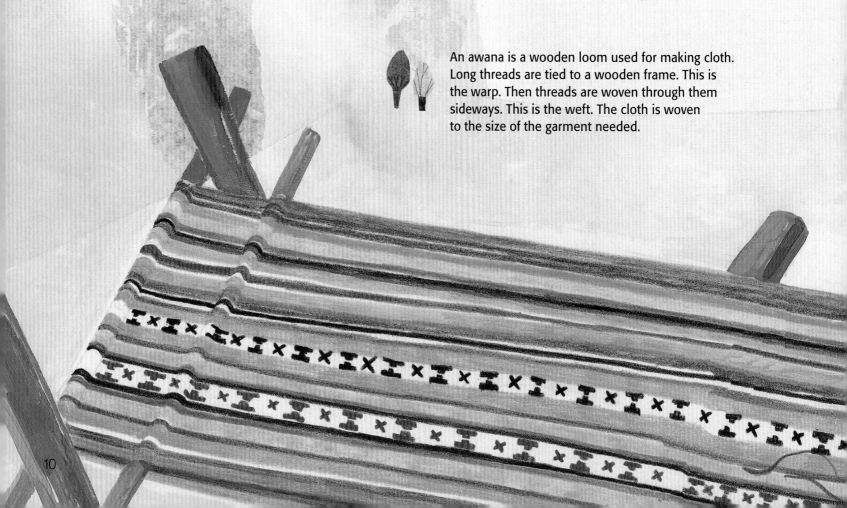

Yana woke up her father
who was taking an afternoon nap.
"Dad, I wanted to help Usco and Mom
but they don't need me.
Can I help you to get ready
for the Festival of the Sun?"

Her father yawned. "It's okay.
You can have fun instead."
Then he went back to sleep.

It was the day before the festival.
Dad practiced what he needed to do
as king of the festival. He said,
"Inca forever!" and his voice shook.

"Dad, your voice is all wobbly!"
Yana told him. "You should say it louder."

Her father smiled at her.
"Honey, why don't you go and play?"

It was the day of the Festival of the Sun.
Cuzco Square was crowded with people.
Yana's family followed the parade
to the hill for the final ceremony.

Yana's heart thumped at the thought
of seeing her father as the festival king.

18

Flags were stuck on the walls.
Torches flamed when they were lit.
There were long lines of soldiers,
and lines of ladies dancing.
People were taking photos.
Yana stood on her tiptoes
to try to see her father.

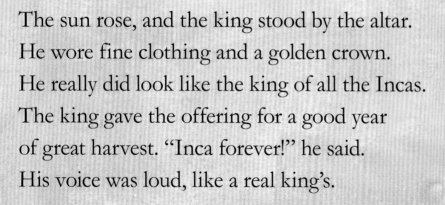

The sun rose, and the king stood by the altar.
He wore fine clothing and a golden crown.
He really did look like the king of all the Incas.
The king gave the offering for a good year
of great harvest. "Inca forever!" he said.
His voice was loud, like a real king's.

Once the offering was burnt
and the smoke rose toward the sun,
the sacrifice was finished.
The king blessed all the people there.

In the Festival of the Sun, the person
playing the king offers the heart of
a llama – which is an animal like
an alpaca but larger – to the sun god.

When Dad saw Yana, he strode toward her.
Yana felt shy. She looked down at her feet.
Dad picked her up and spun her around.
"Yana! My own dear daughter!"

Yana's shyness turned into a smile.
She felt like an Incan princess.

Traditional music flowed in the marketplace
and people danced joyfully to cheerful rhythms.

Every year is revived in this Incan way.
Even when Yana is a grandmother,
the Festival of the Sun will continue.

The Sun Nation That Still Cherishes the Inca Culture

The flag of Peru is red and white. On the middle of the white section is the Peruvian coat of arms with the three national symbols of Peru: the llama, the quina tree and a cornucopia of gold. The cornucopia of gold represents the nation's prosperity.

The Festival of the Sun, Inti Raymi

One of the great festivals of South America, the Festival of the Sun began when people prayed to the sun god for a great harvest. Every year in Cuzco, the Festival of the Sun is celebrated, and the person who takes the role of king is called "Inca." Inca means "son of the sun." The festival king is selected from the Peruvian indigenous community, the Quechua tribe. The people of Peru are proud of the Festival of the Sun which is an ongoing part of the Inca tradition.

The Inti Raymi (Festival of the Sun) at an Inca fortress in Cuzco

Inca Empire in the Land of the Sun

The Inca Empire was prosperous from 1438 to 1533, for approximately 100 years. Based in the regions of Peru and Bolivia, it expanded its territory to Ecuador and Chile. Cuzco is the center of Peru politics, economy, and culture, just as it was the capital of the Inca Empire. Cuzco in the Quechua language means "the earth's belly button," or "the center of the world." However, the Inca Empire ended with the Spanish invasion.

Cuzco with the Andres Mountains in the background

The People of the Andes Mountains

The indigenous people of the Andes Mountains live in mud-brick and stone huts, keeping their traditional lifestyle. The men wear hand-woven woollen clothes and ponchos. A poncho is like a seamless cloak with a hole cut for the head. It is also used as a blanket when it is cold.

Quechua children in Cuzco wearing traditional clothing

The Alpaca and the Llama

Alpaca hair is light, soft and warm and is used to make luxury clothing. It is an important export product for Peru. The llama is similar to the alpaca but it is bigger, and its hair is coarser. Llamas are used to carry luggage up the harsh terrain of the Andes Mountains.

27

Lima, the Capital City on the Desert Coast

Lima, the capital city of Peru, is close to the sea.
It was established there by the Spanish because they
needed a port so that their ships could take wealth
from Peru back to Spain. Since the buildings from
those times have been well preserved, Lima has been
recognized as a World Heritage site by UNESCO.
Lima is in a desert area.

Lima, the capital of Peru

Andean Condor, a Bird That Protects the Sky

The Andean condor is the bird that represents Peru.
The indigenous community regard it as a holy creature that links
their gods and humans. There is a saying that when human heroes
die, they are reborn as Andean condors. This bird features
in the Peruvian song, "El Condor Pasa."

Machu Picchu, a Secret City

The ancient Inca city of Machu Picchu is on a mountain ridge
in the south-central area of the Andes Mountains.
It is called "sky city" because it cannot be seen from the valley below.
On top of the mountain are many buildings made from finely cut stone,
which lock together without needing cement. How the Inca people made
these elaborate buildings is not known.

The Machu Picchu site, north-west of Cuzco, located in the Urubamba area.

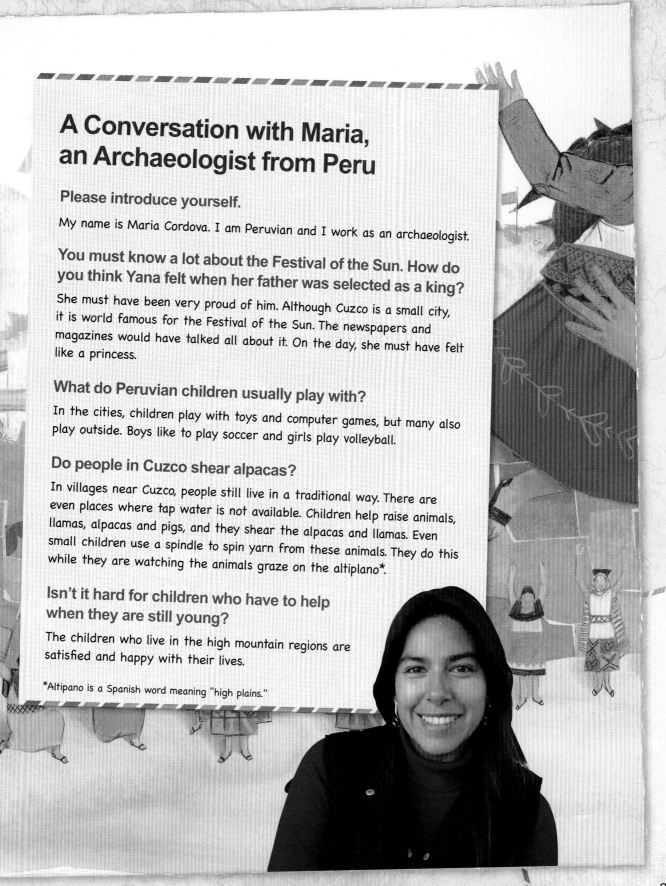

A Conversation with Maria, an Archaeologist from Peru

Please introduce yourself.

My name is Maria Cordova. I am Peruvian and I work as an archaeologist.

You must know a lot about the Festival of the Sun. How do you think Yana felt when her father was selected as a king?

She must have been very proud of him. Although Cuzco is a small city, it is world famous for the Festival of the Sun. The newspapers and magazines would have talked all about it. On the day, she must have felt like a princess.

What do Peruvian children usually play with?

In the cities, children play with toys and computer games, but many also play outside. Boys like to play soccer and girls play volleyball.

Do people in Cuzco shear alpacas?

In villages near Cuzco, people still live in a traditional way. There are even places where tap water is not available. Children help raise animals, llamas, alpacas and pigs, and they shear the alpacas and llamas. Even small children use a spindle to spin yarn from these animals. They do this while they are watching the animals graze on the altiplano*.

Isn't it hard for children who have to help when they are still young?

The children who live in the high mountain regions are satisfied and happy with their lives.

*Altipano is a Spanish word meaning "high plains."

Pacific Ocean

Peru

Name: Republic of Peru

Location: North-central region of South America

Area: 798,586 mi² (1,285,200 km²)

Capital: Lima

Population: Approx. 29.99 million (2012)

Language: Spanish, Quechua

Religion: Catholicism (Christianity)

Main exports: Natural minerals, marine products, textiles, chemicals, farm products

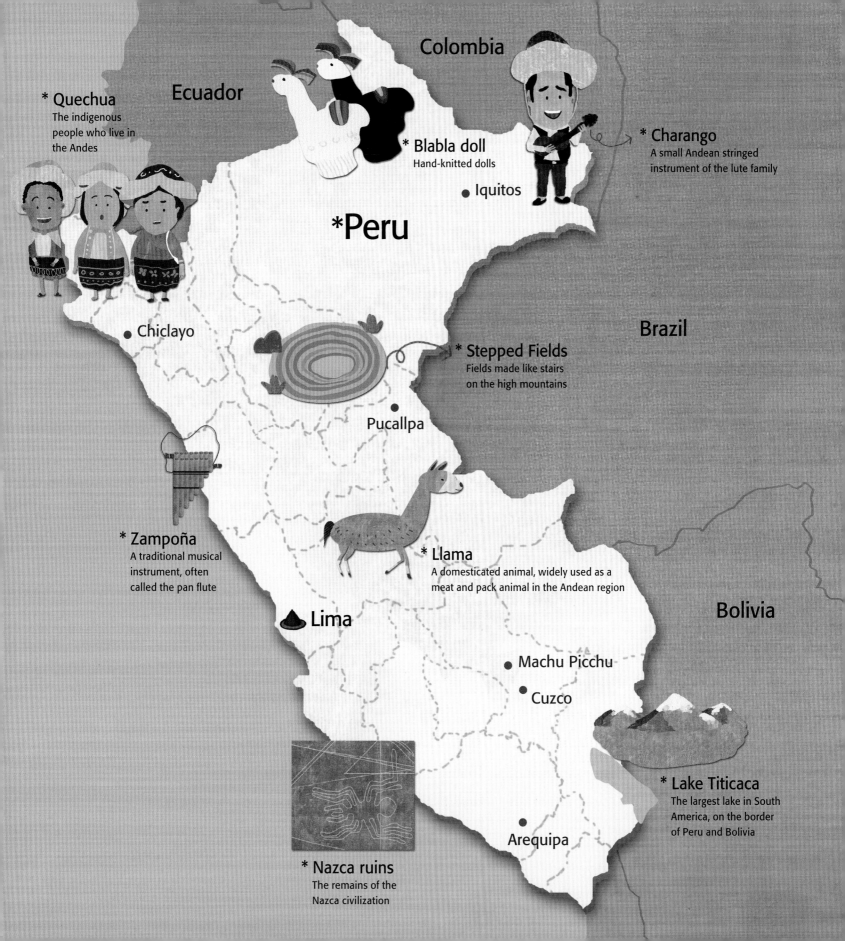

Colombia

Ecuador

* Quechua
The indigenous
people who live in
the Andes

* Blabla doll
Hand-knitted dolls

* Charango
A small Andean stringed
instrument of the lute family

*Peru

Iquitos

Brazil

Chiclayo

* Stepped Fields
Fields made like stairs
on the high mountains

Pucallpa

* Zampoña
A traditional musical
instrument, often
called the pan flute

* Llama
A domesticated animal, widely used as a
meat and pack animal in the Andean region

Bolivia

Lima

Machu Picchu

Cuzco

* Lake Titicaca
The largest lake in South
America, on the border
of Peru and Bolivia

Arequipa

* Nazca ruins
The remains of the
Nazca civilization

Original Korean text by Jong-soon Jo
Illustrations by Sinae Jo
Korean edition © Aram Publishing

This English edition published by big & SMALL in 2016
by arrangement with Aram Publishing
English text edited by Joy Cowley
English edition © big & SMALL 2016

Distributed in the United States and Canada by
Lerner Publishing Group, Inc.
241 First Avenue North
Minneapolis, MN 55401 U.S.A.
www.lernerbooks.com

Images by page no. - left to right, top to bottom
Page 26: © Mme Berthe (GFDL); Page 27: © Martin St-Amant (CC-BY-3.0);
© Rod Waddington from Kergunyah, Australia (CC-BY-SA-2.0);
Page 28: all images public domain; Page 29: public domain

ISBN: 978-1-925247-51-0

Printed in Korea